YOUR KNOWLEDGE HAS VALUE

Effective Data Mining Techniques for Unstructured Data in Big Data

Dnyandeo Khemnar

Bibliographic information published by the German National Library:

The German National Library lists this publication in the National Bibliography; detailed bibliographic data are available on the Internet at http://dnb.dnb.de.

ISBN: 9783346783400
This book is also available as an ebook.

© GRIN Publishing GmbH
Nymphenburger Straße 86
80636 München

Print and binding: Books on Demand GmbH, Norderstedt, Germany
Printed on acid-free paper from responsible sources.

The present work has been carefully prepared. Nevertheless, authors and publishers do not incur liability for the correctness of information, notes, links and advice as well as any printing errors.

GRIN web shop: https://www.grin.com/document/1307474

"Effective Data Mining Technique use with Structured and Unstructured data of Big Data"

Dnyandeo S. Khemnar

Table of Contents

1. INTRODUCTION

There is an increasing need for sharing data that contain personal information from distributed databases. For example, in the healthcare domain, a national agenda to develop the Nationwide Health Information Network (NHIN) to share information among hospitals and other providers and support appropriate use of health information beyond direct patient care with privacy protection. Privacy preserving data analysis, and data publishing have received considerable attention in recent years as promising approaches for sharing data while preserving individual privacy.

Main goal is to publish an anonymized view of integrated data, T, which will be immune to attacks(fig1.1). Attacker runs the attack, i.e. a single or a group of external or internal entities that wants to breach privacy of data using background knowledge. Collaborative data publishing is carried out successfully with the help of trusted third party (TTP), which guarantees that information or data about particular individual is not disclosed anywhere, that means it maintains privacy. Here it is assumed that the data providers are semi honest. A more desirable approach for collaborative data publishing is, first aggregate then anonymize (fig 1) [1].

In fig 1.1, T1, T2, T3 and T4 are databases for which data is provided by provider like provider P1 provides data for database T1. These distributed data coming from different providers get aggregate by TTP (trusted third party) or using SMC protocol. Then these aggregated data anonymized further by any anonimization technique. P0 is the authenticate user and P1 trying to breach privacy of data which is provided by other users with the help of BK (Background knowledge). This type of attack we can call as a "insider attack". We have to protect our system from such a type of attacks

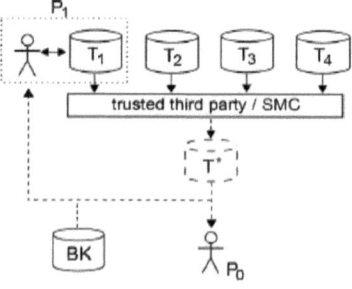

Fig1.1: Aggregate and Anonymize

1

1.1 IDEA AND MOTIVATION

In this era large amount of data are getting shared throughout world. So privacy preserving data publishing has been studied extensively in recent years. This data may contain private data like personal information of any person, household or an organization that should not be disclosed to other have to protect. To maintain the security some privacy preservation techniques are available. Privacy preservation techniques are mainly used to reduce the leakage of formation.

Now a days for anonymization of data from multiple data providers by using techniques like generalization for k anonymity and bucketization for maintaining L diversity are getting studied. In these techniques, the information have to protect can call as a sensitive attribute (SA) i.e. disease of patient, salary of employee etc. The second part of any database is identifier (ID) i.e. name and third is quasi identifier (QI) i.e. age, zip code etc. But these techniques have some disadvantages like data lose , membership disclosure etc. Existing system[1] is depends on providers and is used generalization technique for anonymization. This will increase in data loss. To avoid this we studied slicing technique.

1.2 LITERATURE SURVEY

In this section we are presenting the different methods which are previously used for anonymization. We discuss some advantages and limitation of these systems.

C. Dwork in his survey result [2] of differential privacy, evaluates and summarize different approaches to privacy preserving data publishing (PPDP), study of different challenges in practically publishing of data, clarify the other related problems which are different from PPDP and requirements that make PPDP different from others and proposed future research directions. They identify the research direction in PPDP like privacy preserving tools for individuals, privacy protection in emerging technology and incorporation of privacy protection and engineering process.

N. Mohammed, B. C. M. Fung, P. C. K. Hung, and C. Lee, proposed LKC privacy model for high dimensional relational data for healthcare system[3]. This LKC model gives better result than traditional k anonymization model. But LKC model consider only relational data and healthcare data is complex, may be a combination of relational data, transaction data and textual data.

Two party protocol DPP2GA is presented by authors W. Jiang and C. Clifton which is two party protocol[4]. Only k anonymity is not sufficient to preserve privacy. Hence this this protocol helps in it but major disadvantages of DPP2GA is it may not produce a precise data when data are not partitioned. It is only privacy preserving protocol not SMC because it introduce certain inference problem.

W. Ziang and C. Clifton presented a two party framework DkA[5]. This helps to maintaining a benefits of partitioning of data while generating integrated k anonymous data. This is proven to generate k anonymous dataset and satisfying security definition of SMC. But DkA is not a multiparty framework.

A. Machanavajjhala, J. Gehrke, D. Kifer, and M. Venkitasubramaniam proposed a system with diversity[6]. This system provides a security over k anonymity. Attacker can attack on anonymized system with the help of BK(background knowledge). L diversity helps to overcome this problem.

New system which helps for anonymization is slicing[10]. This is very useful technique for high dimentional data. But there could be a loss of data utility

2. PROBLEM DEFINITION AND SCOPE

Problem definition: Our main goal is to publish an anonymized view of integrated data, P* which will be immune to attacks. We improve the security and privacy with the help of slicing technique which fulfil privacy verification with better performance than provider aware (base algorithm) and encryption algorithm.

2.1 SCOPE

○ Proposed system is run on LAN network.

○ Distributed system like hospital patient data management, companies employers salary account management system, banking system like personal information of account holders etc where we need to secure collaborative data

2.2 SOFTWARE CONTEXT

Mantaining security and privacy of document without using encryptiom have been a challenging problem in distributed network. Various methods and strategies are developed to make maximum probability to make it possible. In this project, a method is proposed and implemented to improve the reliability and computation time.

2.3 SOFTWARE CONSTRAINTS

- Experiment graph is calculated for computation time against any encryption algorithm and provider aware algorithm i.e existing system algorithm. If OS system change result may change as efficiency, throughput of system may change.
- Proposed algorithm is designed for LAN connection.

2.4 OUTCOMES

Output data table shows secure data publishing which provide privacy to sensitive attribute.

Comparison shows the computation time difference between encryption algorithm , provider aware algorithm and slicing with data privacy algorithm.

2.5 HARDWARE SPECIFICATION

- Processor - Pentium –IV

- Speed - 1.1 Ghz

- RAM - 256 MB(min)

- Hard Disk - 20 GB

2.6 S/W SPECIFICATION

- Operating System - Windows7/8

- Programming Language- Java

- Tool – NetBeans 7.1:

NetBeans IDE provides first-class comprehensive support for the newest Java technologies and latest Java enhancements before other IDEs. It is the first IDE providing support for JDK 7, Java EE 7, and JavaFX 2. With its constantly improving Java Editor, many rich features and an extensive range of tools, templates and samples, NetBeans IDE sets the standard for developing with cutting edge technologies out of the box. Keeping a clear overview of large applications, with thousands of folders and files, and millions of lines of code, is a daunting task. NetBeans IDE provides different views of your data, from multiple project windows to helpful tools for setting up your applications and managing them efficiently

2.7 AREA OF DISSERTATION

Collaborative distributed database system

3. DISSERTATION PLAN

3.1 PROJECT PLAN

This plan is the basis for the execution and tracking of all the project activities. It shall be used throughout the life of the project and shall be kept up to date to reflect the actual accomplishments and plans of the project.

Fig 3.1 shows the software project plan. Requirement gathering and plan for the initial part of the project was as follows:

While requirement gathering and analysis of proposed system we to understand the problem definition and reliability of system. It also includes gathering information about required software and hardware. These explains in chapter 1 and 2.

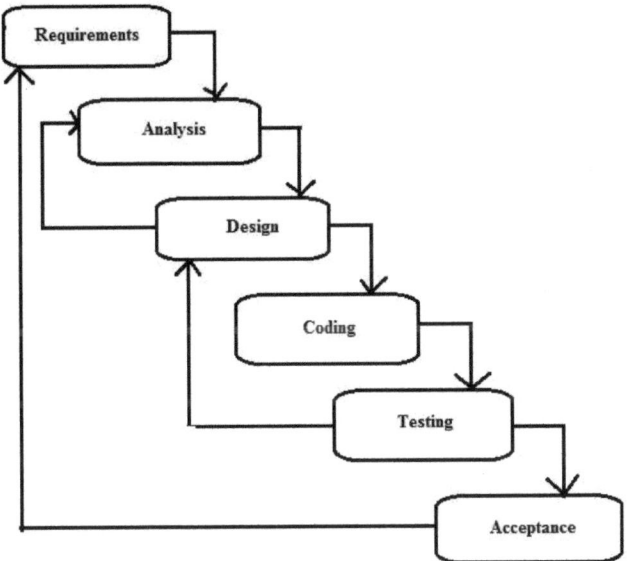

Fig 3.1 project plan

In designing phase we have to prepare preliminary design of overall work flow of project which will explain further. Coding is nothing but the development part of the system. For coding study algorithms include in chapter 5 and use reliable s/w and h/w for better performance.

Last but not least part of development is testing. There are many testing approaches are available. Testing will help to decide whether our system fulfills our requirements or not. In chapter 6 we explain some parameters of testing. If testing gives proper result it will go for user acceptance. If any change accurse whole plan will gat repeat.

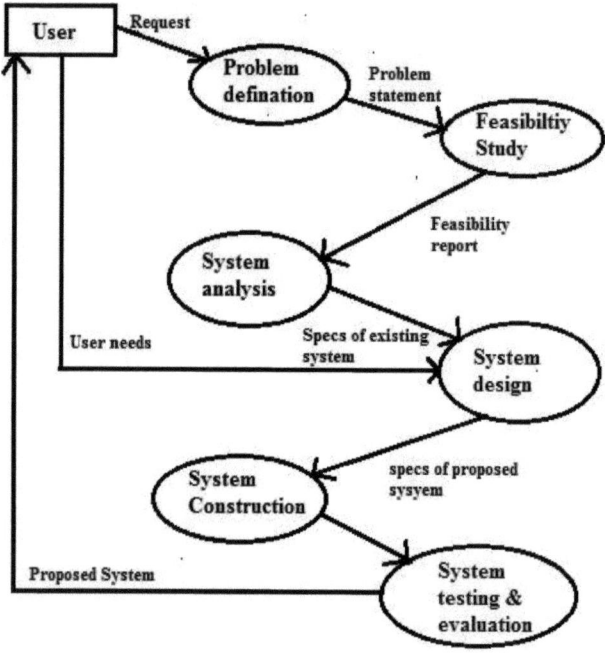

Fig 3.2 software development lifecycle

3.2 TIMELINE OF PROJECT

Project planning is a form of operational planning, whereby the consecutive steps to implement the project activities are carefully mapped out, based on an analysis of relevant information and linked to the program in which the project takes place and to which it should contribute. Essentially, the project planning involves establishing the scope, aims and objectives of a project, the way in which the project will be performed, the roles and responsibilities of those involved and the time and cost estimates.

Table 3.1 Schedule of Project

Month	Schedule	Project Task
December	1st week	Idea about project selection/project topic selection
	3rd week	Submission of project synopsis/Abstract
January	2nd week	First presentation about idea of projects (Feasibility study)
February	3rd & 4th week	Requirement Analysis Preparation
March	1st week	Design of Project-Low level, High level, Data structure, database tables and algorithms.
	3rd week	Presentation with design.
April	1st week	Preparation of preliminary report.
	3rd week	Implementation of first module started.
May	1st week	First module implemented.
	3rd week.	Testing on first module.
June	1st week	Changes in module I if required.
	2nd week	Preparation for module II.
	3rd week	Implementation of second module started.
July	1st week	Second module implemented.
	2nd week	Testing on second module.
July	3rd week	Changes in module II if required.
	4th week	Preparation for module III.
August	1st week	Implementation of third module started.
	4th week	Testing and implementation of third module.

8

September	1st week	Manual testing.
	2nd week	System testing.
	3rd week	Performance testing.
	4th week	Security testing.
	1st & 2nd week	Improvement according to testing
	3rd & 4th week	Testing for acceptance

3.3 FEASIBILITY STUDY

Software projects are bind to delivery dates and available resources. Hence by doing feasibility study we have to determine whether the system would be feasible or not.

3.3.1 Economical Feasibility

It is a cost/benefit analysis. For implementing proposed system there is no need to upgrade large number of hardware and software. By installing netbeans, JDK etc we can develop a system. These software's are easily available with lowest cost.

3.3.2 Technical Feasibility

It developed system performs well, then it is technically feasible. The technical issue usually raised during the feasibility stage of the investigation includes the following:

- Does the necessary technology exist or not?
- Do the proposed equipment have the technical capacity to hold the data required to use the new system?
- Can the system be upgraded in future?
- Are there technical guarantees of accuracy, reliability, ease of access and data security?

Our system is technically feasible. The technology we used as specify in h/w and s/w specification are easily available and reliable technologies . The technical concept like buchetization, permutation, anonymization, L diversity can understand properly. This developed system have some future enhancement which we explain in chapter 7 and that can upgraded. The analysis about accuracy, reliability, ease of access and data security, this system

9

can reach upto 90% satisfaction. Because there might be a data loss or if lot of data contains same sensitive attribute like disease which we have to secure then system may fails. But this is rare situation. Operational feasibility is a measure of how well a proposed system solves the problems.

3.3.3 Operational feasibility

Our proposed work maintains the privacy and security on data publishing with minimum computation time. As explain earlier our problem statement is to publish the anonymized view of data maintaining the security and privacy of sensitive attribute. Our proposed system solves this problem. In chapter 8 we will discuss the outcome and performance which proves that our system fulfill operational feasibility

3.3.4 Time Feasibility

Time feasibility is the parameter which measure whether the system get completed within time or not? Whether the systems computation time is considerable or not?

Our systems computation time is less than any encryption algorithm. In chapter 8 we discuss the performance regarding computation time and time complexity of our system. Our system completes development within desired time. This shows that our system fulfills time feasibility

3.4 RISK MANAGEMENT

The identification of Risk is central to the success and failure of the project, hence I have made a concentrated effort to minimize and even eliminate certain risk related to project.

3.4.1 Project Risk:

For our proposed system we find out risk by giving answer to the following questions:
1) Is the project scope is stable?
2) Are project requirements are stable?
3) Do all customer/user constituencies agree on the importance of the project and on the requirements for the system/product to be built?

After this analysis we can say following project risk which might be face:

Project scope of this system is stable but small. Due to some advantages like data security, privacy during data publishing in distributed system and it protects data from attacker

10

this system can plays an important role in this area. But the scope of this system is small. If scope increases the system may cause failure. It can cause data loss in certain condition.

3.4.2 Risk Assessment

Table 3.2 Risk Assessment

Risk Type	Risk	Impact
Schedule Risk	Unexpected project scope expansions	Critical
	Resources are not tracked properly	Medium
Programmatic Risks	Logical errors	Critical
	Runtime exception	Medium
	Global and local declaration	Low

3.5 EFFORT AND COST ESTIMATION

3.5.1 Lines of code (LOC)

Project Estimation report is size oriented matrix. Here, constructive cost model i.e. COCOMO is used to estimate effort and time duration by using size of software.

Table 3.3 LOC

Sr.No	Module	LOC
1	Admin	1432
2	Doctor	1204
3	Slicing	996
4	Provider aware	546
5	DB connection	287
6	Total	4465

3.5.2 Effort

$E=2.4 *(KLOC)^{1.05}$

$= 2.4*4.465^{1.05} = 11.55$

3.5.3 Development Time

The development time in months is calculated by the formula

$D=2.5*(E)^{0.38}$

$=2.5*11.55^{0.38} = 6.33$ appox

3.5.4 Number of People

The recommended number of people is calculated by formula

$N=E/D$

$= 11.55/6.33 = 1.82$ person

4. SOFTWARE REQUIREMENT SPECIFICATION

4.1 INTRODUCTION

The Software Requirement Specification (SRS) document provides a complete description of all requirements, design issues and required specifications against challenges.

4.1.1 Purpose

The purpose of this document is to specify the properties, features and requirements of privacy and security of data in collaborative data publishing in distributed database.

This document includes diagrammatic representation of our system. It includes different forms of diagrams which gives detailed description of our system.

4.1.2 Scope of Document

• Find out flow of system.

• Results will be compared with our expected results.

• check performance analysis to prove the feasibility of our problem statement

4.1.3 Overview of responsibilities of developer

The responsibilities from developer perspective are to develop the application as per the requirement with user friendly user interface. For this the developer is required to go through the concepts required to be implemented. The developer follows the software design life cycle, starting from requirement gathering, analysis, design, coding, and then implementation of the system. After the implementation is completed, the simulation generated is tested manually for random topology having random number of nodes and varying packet size.

4.2 PRODUCT OVERVIEW

In this project, the main aim to avoid congestion and increase reliability in an event driven WSN. This involves creation of random topology, generation of event; the nodes which are near the event area will detect the event and then forms an atomic decision and broadcast their packet to Mobile data collector node. The node will follow random path to collect the data packet and disseminate it towards the sink node.

13

4.2.1 Block diagram

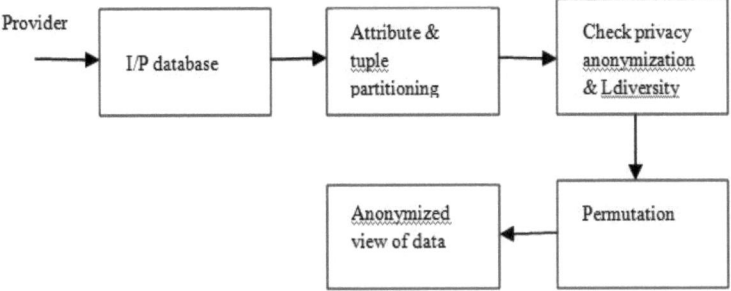

Fig 4.1: Proposed system

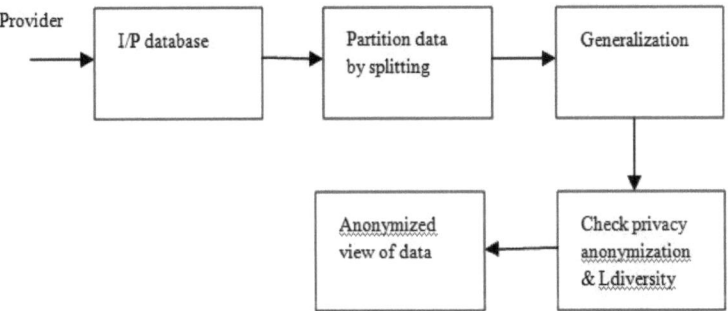

Fig 4.2: Existing base system

4.3 FUNCTINAL MODEL

4.3.1 Flow diagram

A diagram showing the flow of information through the function and the transformation it undergoes is presented.

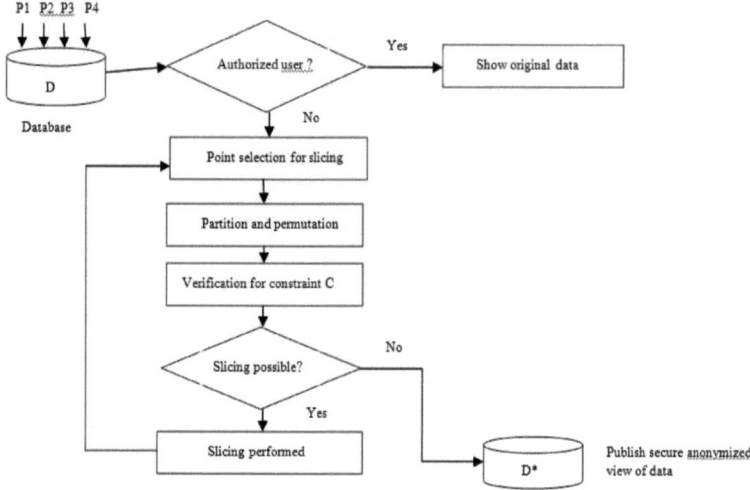

Fig 4.3: Flow diagram

4.3.2 Data Flow Diagram

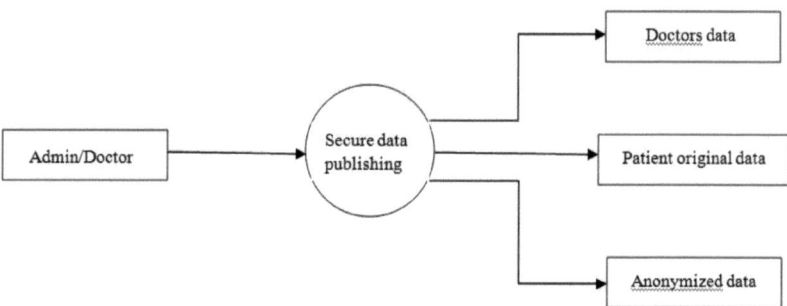

Fig 4.4: DFD level 0

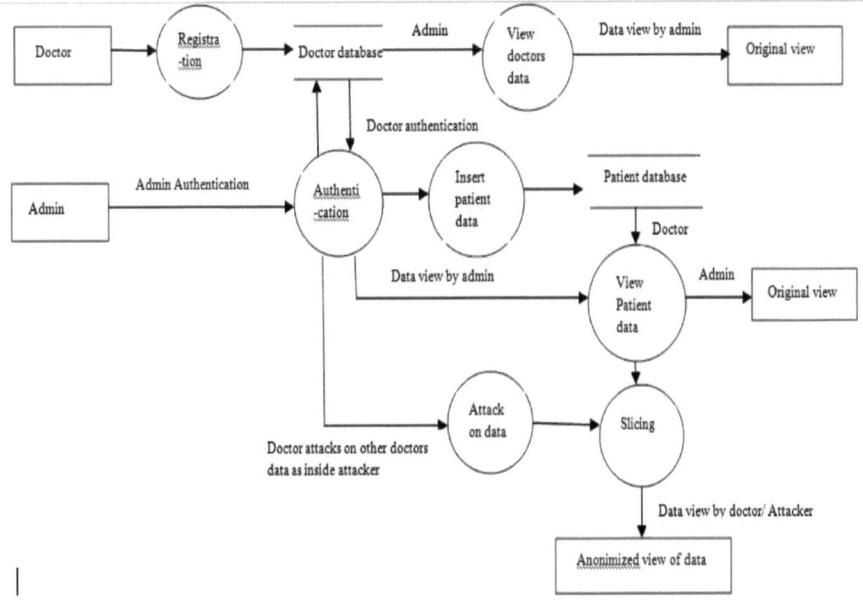

Fig 4.5: DFD level 1

4.3.3 UML Diagrams

The unified modeling language(UML) is a graphical language for visualization, specifying, constructing and documenting the artifact of a software intensive system.

The UML gives a stanrderd was to write systems blue prints, covering conceptual things, such as business processes and system functions.

4.3.3.1 Sequence diagram

A Sequence diagram is an interaction diagram that emphasizes the time ordering of messages. Interaction diagram shows that interaction consisting of a set of objects and their relationships including messages that may be dispatched among them.

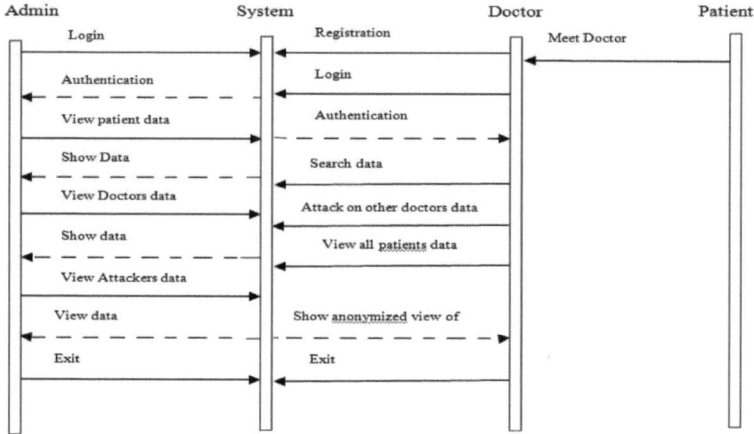

Fig 4.6: Sequence diagram

4.3.3.2 Class diagram

Class diagram gives different classes and their relationships with each other. It is one of the structural UML diagram.

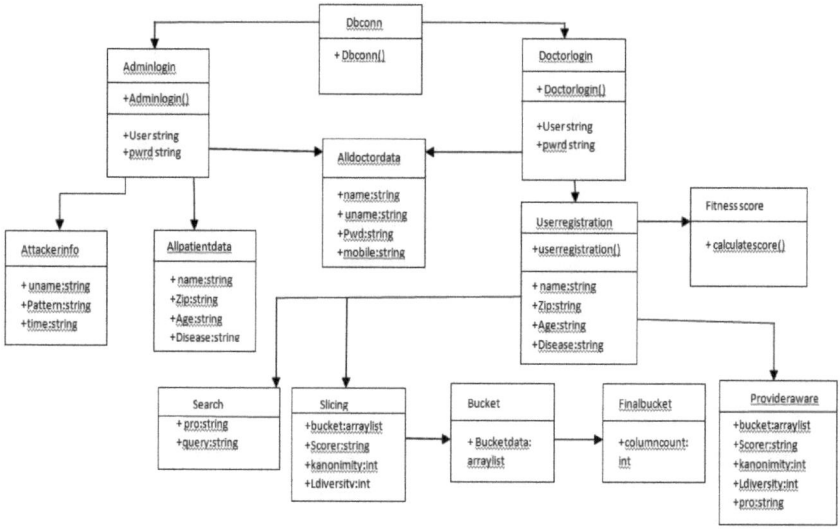

Fig 4.7: Class diagram

4.3.4 Non-Functional Requirements

The application should be efficient and self-adaptable.

4.4 BEHAVIORAL MODEL AND DESCRIPTION

This section gives the description about behavior of the software.

4.4.1 Description of software behavior

The major functions and states are:

Functions: 1) generation of anonymized view of data

        2) Detection of attacks

        3) Analysis of data

States: 1) Input given to system for slicing

        2) Check for privacy constraint and if slicing possible run the loop

        3) Output will in anonymized view

4.4.2 Use case diagram

Use case diagram represents the actors and procedures belongs to that actors in system.

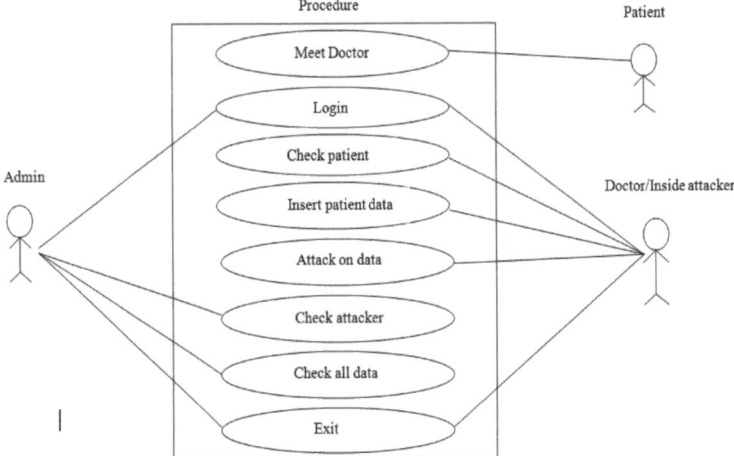

Fig 4.8: use case diagram

18

5.   DETAILED DESIGN

A design document is a stable reference to the high level design of data, architecture, interface and component for the software. This document aims at guiding any other developer about the development of the application as per the requirement. It will help other developer to enhance the system for future scope. The project is mainly concerned to implement an algorithm that fulfills our problem definition.

5.1 ARCHITECTURE DESIGN

This document includes detailed description of flow of architecture and algorithms which is used to develop this system. It will help to other developer as well as to same developer for future study.

Consider Fig. 4.1 shows our proposed system in which input data is given from different provider. Select point for slicing. Check that input data against privacy constraint C for data privacy Check further is slicing is possible or not. If it possible for input data perform slicing. Our final output are also anonymized data(D*). Any adversary(coalition of data users with data providers cooperating to breach privacy of anonymized records) cannot breach privacy of data. In this system we are using horizontal as well as vertical partitioning over database. For detailed design following modules are consider.

5.1.1 Algorithms:

1.Anonymization by slicing:

Slicing is basically depends on Attribute and tuple partitioning. In Attribute partitioning (vertical partition) we partitioned data as {name},{age-zip} and {Disease} and tuple partitioning (horizontal partition) as {t1,t2,t3,t4,t5,t6}. In attribute partitioning age and zip are partitioned together because they both are highly correlated because they are quasi identifiers (QI). These QI can be known to attacker. While tuple partitioning system should check L diversity for the sensitive attribute (SA) column. Algorithm runs are as follows.

1. Initialize bucket k=n, int i= rowcount, column count=C, Q={D}, // D= data into database, Arraylist= a[i];
2. While Q is not empty
    If i<=n
        Check L diversity;

19

Else

  i++;

  Return D*;

3. Q=Q-{D*+a[i]};

4. Repeat step 2 and 3 with next tuple in Q

5. D*=D*U A[D] // next anonymized view of data D

First initialize k = limit of data anonymization bucket size, number of rows, number of columns, array list and database in the queue(step 1). Further process will done if and only if queue is not empty i.e there should be data in database. Check data for L diversity if rowcount = k = m (step 2). Initially Q= Queue of data. If our bucket data fulfill k anonymity and L diversity, it return D* i.e anonymized view of data. The data from the database which cannot fulfill requirement of privacy will stored in array list a[i]. Now data remains in database i.e in Q = Q-{D*+ a[i]} (step 3). Repeat step 2 and step 3. A[D] is anonymization of data in database. Apply above steps for remaining data and create new anonymization view which is the union of original view and new one i.e D* = D*UA[D].

2. L diversity: L diversity is the concept of maintaining uniqueness within data. In this system we used this concept on SA i.e on disease. Our anonymized bucket size is 6 and I maintain L=4 i.e from 6 disease record 4 must be unique.

1. Initialize L=m, int i;

2. If i= n-m+1;

  Then a[0].....a[1], insert these values as they are in Q;

  i++;

3. Else

  Check privacy constraint for every incremented value in Q

 If

  L=n then

  Fscore=1

  Insert value in the row

  i++;

 else

  Add element to arraylist a[i];

4. Exit

First initialize L=m and rowcount i. If i=n-m+1 i.e if k=n=6 and L=m=4 then i=3, upto third row data doesn't need to check for Fscore. Add this data as they are coming from Q (step 1 and 2). For further data from Q check data for privacy constraint. If data fulfills L , then Fscore=1. If data doesn't fulfill Fscore=1, then add element in array list a[i] (step 3).

3.Permutation: Permutation means rearrangement of records of data. In my project. I used permutation process for rearrangement of quasi identifier i.e {Zip-Age}

4.Fscore: Fscore is privacy fitness score i.e the level of fulfillment of privacy constraint C. If fscore=1 then C(D*)= true.

5. Constraint C: C is a privacy constraint in which D* should fulfill slicing condition with L diversity as explain above. Consider value of L diversity is 4. Fscore should be 1 when system fulfills L diversity condition.

Some verification processes are carried out.
1) Verification for L diversity: For verification of L diversity I used Fitness score function. For checking L diversity generate continuous similar values of SA i.e insert similar disease. Check for Fscore=1. If L=m, return Fscore. If privacy breach i.e if anonymized view take data as insertad then it breached privacy. D* shoud take data which fulfill L= m.

1. Generate continuous similar values of SA
2. Check for privacy constaint and fscore=1;
3. If
        Privacy breach;
        Then early stop;
   Else
        Return (Fscore);
4. Exit

2) Verification for strength of system against number of provider: For verification against number of provider, add one more attribute in anonymized data as a provider to output. This verification will prove that our technique of anonymization doesn't depend on number of provider. Existing system[1] i.e provider aware anonymization algorithm depends on database as well as provider.

1. Generate values of SA by providers P= 1.....n
2. Check for privacy constraint and Fscore=1 with respect to number of provider
3. If

       Privacy breach;

       Then early stop;

Else

       Return(Fscore);

4. Exit

5.2 INTERFACES

5.2.1 Human Interface

This shows that how our proposed system start communication with user.

5.2.2. Database interface

This shows that how our proposed system start communication with database.

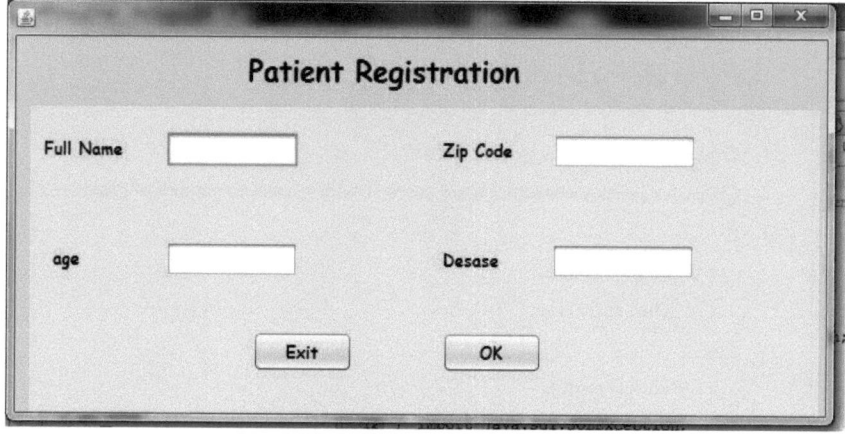

6.   TESTING

Test Specification document is used to provide the test plan for proposed system. It provides the details about testing to be carried out on the application. It includes all the testing strategies and methods which are decided for the application as per the test plan. Testing may include white box testing, black box, Performance testing, system testing etc.

6.1 INTRODUCTION

It provides an overview of the entire test strategies to be tested on application. It describes both the test plan and the test procedure. The testing of application is depends on:

1) The number of nodes required for the distributed system.
2) Operating system used.
3) Efficiency and reliability of system and network.

6.1.1 Goals and Objective

Overall goal and objective of the test process are as follows:

1. Improve the Reliability of proposed system
2. Reduce the computation time and
3. Maximize the security of private data.

6.2 TESTING STRATEGY

6.2.1 White Box Testing

Sometimes called glass-box testing is a test case design method that uses the control structure of the procedural design to derive test cases. Using white-box testing methods, the software engineer can derive test cases that (1) guarantee that all independent paths within a module have been exercised at least once, (2) exercise all logical decisions on their true and false sides, (3) execute all loops at their boundaries and within their operational bounds, and (4) exercise internal data structures to ensure their validity. White-box testing of software is predicated on close examination of procedural detail by unit and integration testing. Providing test cases that exercise specific sets of conditions and/or loops tests logical paths through the software. The status of the program may be examined at various points to determine if the expected or asserted status corresponds to the actual status. Basis path testing is a white-box testing technique first proposed by Tom McCabe. The basis path method enables the test case designer to derive a logical complexity measure of a procedural design and use this measure as a guide for defining a basis set of execution paths. Test cases derived to exercise the basis set are guaranteed to execute every statement in the program at least one time during testing.

24

In this system, the system was tested for the calculation matters were the data provided for giving the right output or not. If wrong data was provided then what it is throwing error or accepting.

6.2.2 Black Box Testing

Also called behavioral testing, focuses on the functional requirements of the software. That is, black box testing enables the software engineer to derive sets of input conditions that will fully exercise all functional requirements for a program. Black box testing is not an alternative to white-box techniques. Rather, it is a complementary approach that is likely to uncover a different class of error than white-box methods. When computer software is considered, black box testing Alludes to tests that are conducted at the software interface. Although they are designed to uncover errors, black-box tests are used to demonstrate that software functions are operational, that input is properly accepted and output is correctly produced and that the integrity of external information is maintained. A black-box test examines some fundamental aspect of a system with a little regard for the internal logical structure of the software. Black-box testing attempts to find errors in the following categories:

1. Incorrect or missing functions
2. Interface errors
3. Errors in data structures or external database access
4. Behavior or performance errors
5. Initialization and termination errors

By applying back-box techniques, a set of test cases that satisfy the following criteria are derived:

☐ Test cases that reduce, by a count that is greater than one, the number of additional test cases that must be designed to achieve reasonable testing.

☐ Test cases that tell us something about the presence or absence of classes of errors, rather than an error associated only with the specific test at hand.

White-box testing should not, however, be dismissed as impractical. A limited number of important logical paths can be selected and exercised. Important data structures can be probed for validity. The attributes of both black and white box testing can be combined to provide an approach that validates the software interface and selectively ensures that the internal workings of the software are correct. Black box testing for this system was done to check the internal testing i.e., the system is working properly in each case or no. What kind of errors are there in database design. To find out faults, mistakes there is use of different black box testing methods like system testing, performance testing, load testing, etc.

6.2.3 System testing

System testing is testing the whole system. It follows the scope of black box testing which doesn't require any knowledge of design of code or logic. It performs to test the fulfillment of functional requirement specification (FRS) and software requirement specification (SRS). It tests about graphical user interface, usability, performance, compatibility, exception handling, load, volume, stress, security, accessibility, failure and recovery etc.

6.2.4 Performance testing

Any software should be a quality software and quality measures by using the attributes reliability, scalability and resource usage. Performance testing is the general testing which determine how system performs? This is in terms of responsiveness and stability under maximum workload.

Proposed system gives positive response to performance testing. It works properly and give proper output for large number of database. Resource usage is also maximum. The only thing is for very large amount of database system performance i.e computation time of system get increased.

Table 6.1 analyses some test cases which tests our software according to above testing strategies and shows up to which extent our software fulfill requirement.

Table 6.1 Test Cases.

Test case ID	Flow	Expected Result	Actual Result
1	User Login	Allow login to authenticated user only	System allow login to authenticated user only
2	Insert patient data	Patient data should properly inserted into database	Patient data should properly inserted into database
3	Attack by doctor as a inside attacker	Should give anonymized view of data pblishing that fulfill SA privacy	give anonymized view of data pblishing that fulfill 90% of SA privacy
4	Search data	Should give attacker information	It gives attacker information if any attacker insert any

			different query
5	Display data	Should display anonymized view of data in table format	Display anonymized view of data in table format
6	Time display	Should give performance time of encryption algorithm and slicing algo	Give performance time of encryption algorithm and slicing algo
7	Error messages	Should give error messages if data is insufficient	Give error messages if data is insufficient
8	Time comparison	Slicing should give less time than blowfish encryption algorithm	Slicing give less computation time than blowfish encryption algorithm

7. DATA TABLE AND DISCUSSION

In this chapter I am going to discuss the input to the system, output given by the system, computation time i.e performance of blowfish encryption system and slicing system and provider aware and slicing system.

7.1 INPUT TO THE SYSTEM

Following table shows the input to the system. The attributes are name, zip, age, and disease.

```
mysql> select * from hospital;
+------------+--------+-----+--------------+---------+
| name       | zip    | age | disease      | provider|
+------------+--------+-----+--------------+---------+
| mark       | 12311  | 45  | cancer       | shila   |
| bob        | 12311  | 34  | cancer       | shila   |
| Alice      | 12311  | 56  | cancer       | shila   |
| pragati    | 23411  | 26  | cold         | pragati |
| sneha      | 23411  | 22  | cold         | subodh  |
| shraddha   | 23411  | 24  | cold         | subodh  |
| Arati      | 34511  | 30  | caugh        | pragati |
| satish     | 34211  | 44  | bp           | subodh  |
| amit       | 54311  | 32  | migrane      | subodh  |
| swamini    | 23422  | 55  | sugar        | pragati |
| shrikant   | 23411  | 45  | attack       | shila   |
| shridhar   | 45322  | 55  | attack       | pragati |
| shiwani    | 23422  | 39  | attack       | shila   |
| shashidhar | 23422  | 60  | attack       | shila   |
| payal      | 34533  | 33  | attack       | shila   |
| a          | 23411  | 56  | high bp      | shila   |
| aa         | 23422  | 54  | bp           | Anand   |
| aaa        | 34211  | 78  | tumour       | Anand   |
| aaaa       | 34211  | 76  | luckemia     | Anand   |
| b          | 12311  | 45  | blood cancer | shila   |
| bb         | 23422  | 56  | flu          | shila   |
| bbb        | 67511  | 56  | flu          | shila   |
| c          | 12322  | 23  | piles        | pragati |
| cc         | 34211  | 32  | tumour       | subodh  |
| pravin     | 269867 | 26  | cough        | NULL    |
+------------+--------+-----+--------------+---------+
25 rows in set (0.00 sec)

mysql>
```

Fig 7.1: Input database

7.2 OUTPUT:

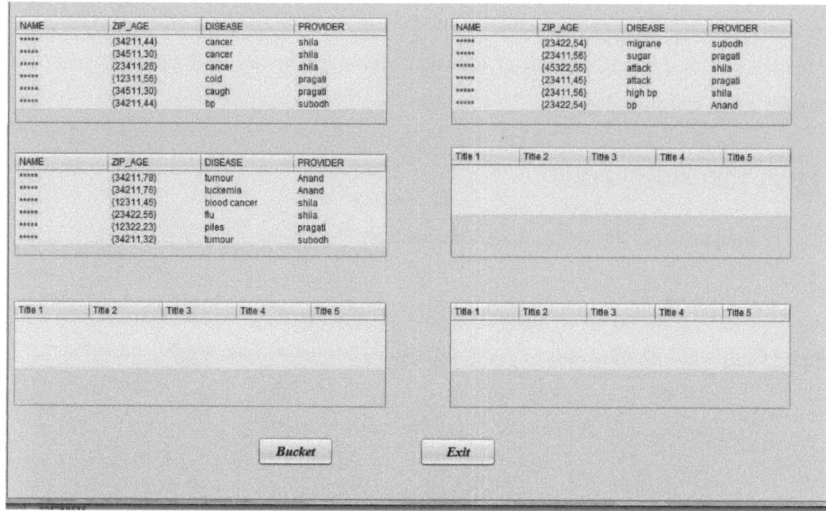

Fig 7.2: Slicing output

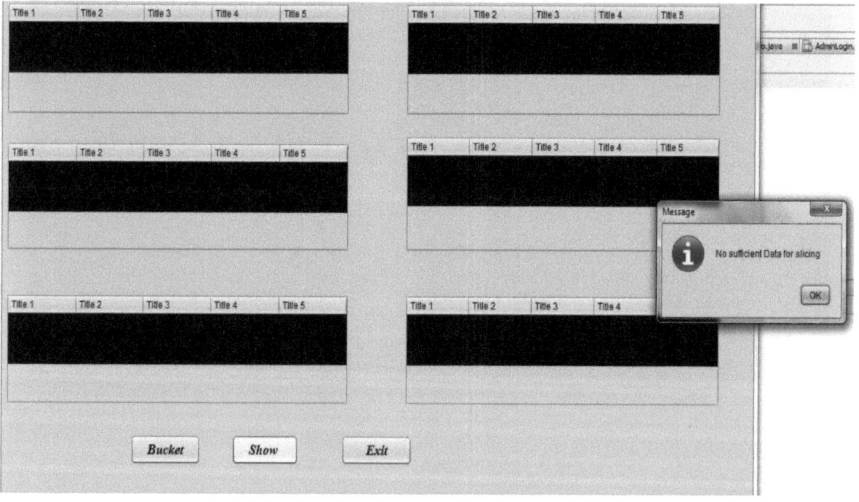

Fig 7.3: Arraylist data output frame

Fig 7.2, it shows the output of the system with computation time of system. From this time we can calculate performance of the system. This output shows the slicing perform on the input data and publish data after checking privacy constraint.

After this operation slicing perform on data store in array list as explain in algorithm of

29

chapter 5. Lost data while fulfilling the privacy condition of slicing will store in an array list. Fig 7.3 shows this.

Many queries are directly affect to the database. These queries can perform delete, alter, drop etc. operation on table. To protect our database from such a query we have to pay attention on the development of system which protects our system against such an attack. Fig 7.4 is the output of such system. When any attacker attacks on system via searching following output will give.

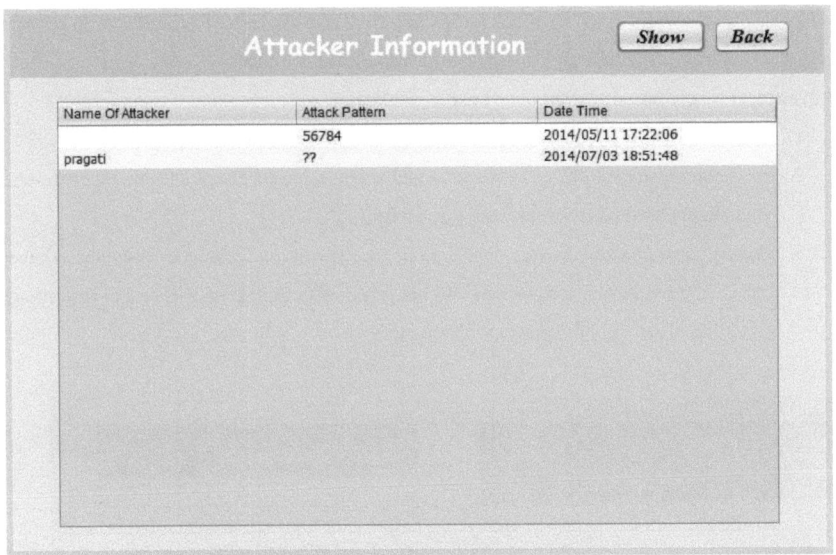

Fig 7.4: Output of attacker information

7.3 PERFORMANCE OF PROPOSED SYSTEM

A measure of a amount of a time required to execute a algorithm is called complexity. To compare different algorithms before deciding on which one have to implement, complexity plays an important role when input are the same and need same output. It expresses the relationship between size of the input and run time of algorithm.

Performance of the system is nothing but the computation time required to run the code. It is depends on coding, platform, compiler, configuration of system and processer. Complexity affects the performance of the system on which a particular algorithm run. But performance doesn't affect the complexity. When two systems give different outputs but basic requirement of systems are same like maintaining security, we can differentiate our system by calculating computation time (execution time) of system.

7.3.1 Performance of proposed system with respect to baseline algorithm:

Fig 7.4 shows the output of the baseline algorithm i.e provider aware algorithm. In this algorithm, while splitting the data it consider providers also. With the help of Mondrian algorithm anonimization takes place. It uses generalization technique and check output for m privacy i.e privacy constraint C. The complexity of provider wawre algorithm which is the recursive process with l diversity check is $O(n^2(logn))$. The complexity of our proposed system is $O(n^2)$. Proposed algorithm uses linear slicing with l diversity check.

Advantages of proposed system over base algorithm:

1. Time complexity of proposed system is less than provider aware algorithm.
2. Base algorithm uses old generalization and suppression techniques for anonymization. And slicing used permutation with l diversity.
3. Base algorithm also consider providers in anonymization technique. If database have only one providers data algorithm will not give any output. Data will loss or in waiting condition. This will not happen with slicing.

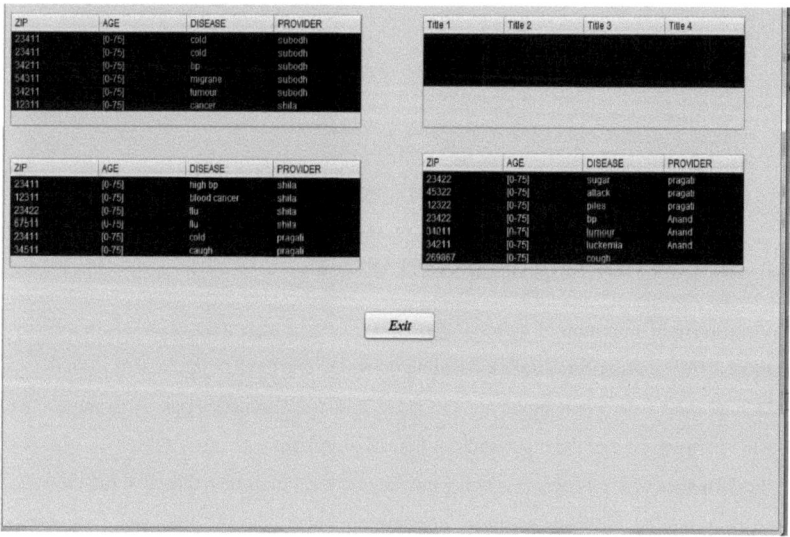

Fig 7.5: output of provider aware algorithm

7.3.2 Performance of proposed system with respect to blowfish encryption algorithm:

Proposed system are used to securely publish data and maintain the privacy of sensitive attribute. Now a days there are many encryption algorithms are available which gives maximum security to attribute. But there computation time is high as compare to this system as shown in graph. We compare proposed algorithm with blowfish encryption algorithm as its performance is better than all other encryption algorithms. If any provider want to send our data to other user, instead of encryption algorithm he can use slicing algorithm. For small scope system like hospital management system where SA is disease or banking sector where SA will be balance of customer.

Advantages of proposed system over encryption algorithm:

1. Major difference are in their computation time.

2. If any attacker knows key then whole data will be decrypt and corrupted. In case of slicing if user send this anonymized data to other user and if attacker will attack on this data, there remain certain probability to maintain privacy.

3. So for some systems we can use anonymization technique in practice instead of encryption algorithm. It will help in increase performance by decreasing computation time of system.

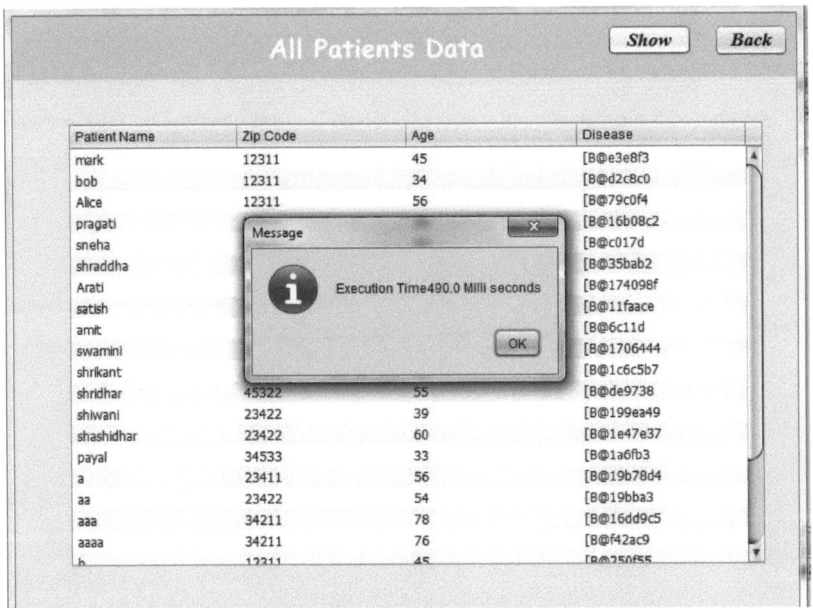

Fig 7.6: output of blowfish algorithm

32

7.4 RESULT

For experiment we consider h/w and s/w configuration as explain in chapter 2.

7.4.1 Difference between proposed algorithm and base algorithm i.e provider aware algorithm:

Input are the number of records in the database. Difference is calculated with respect to complexity as explain in 7.3.1.

Graph 7.1

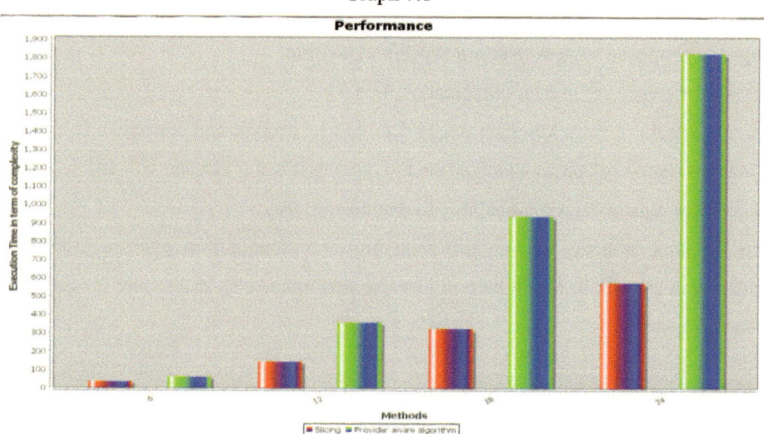

On above 25 records of input (refer 7.1), Graph 2 shows computation time between slicing and encryption algorithm. This shows the performance of the system i.e CPU usage in millisecond of the system on which it runs.

Graph 7.2

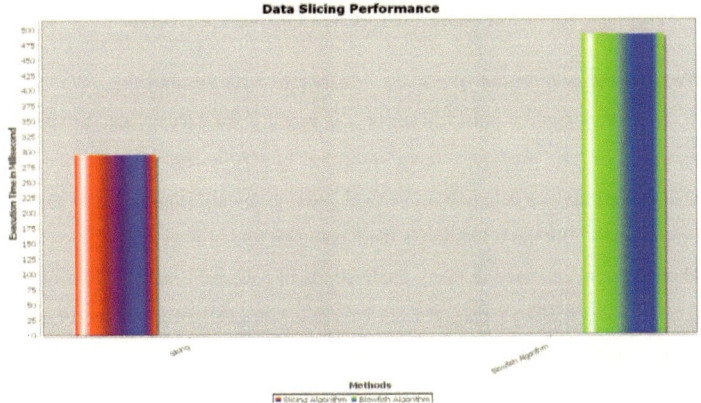

Data Slicing Performance

8.   SUMMARY AND CONCLUSION

We consider a potential attack on collaborative data publishing. We used slicing algorithm for anonymization and L diversity and verify it for security and privacy by using binary algorithm of data privacy. Slicing algorithm is very useful when we are using high dimensional data. It divides data in both vertical and horizontal fashion. Due to encryption we can increase security. But the limitation is there could be loss of data utility.

Above system can used in many applications like hospital management system, many industrial areas where we like to protect a sensitive data like salary of employee. Pharmaceutical company where sensitive data may be a combination of ingredients of medicines, in banking sector where sensitive data is account number of customer, our system can use. It can be used in military area where data is gathered from different sources and need to secured that data from each other to maintain privacy.

This proposed system help to improve the data privacy and security when data is gathered from different sources and output should be in collaborative fashion.

8.1 FUTURE ENHANCEMENT

In future this system can consider for data which are distributed in ad hoc grid computing. Also the system can be consider for set valued data.nThe research work can be follow in the direction that proposed system will be implemented on wireless network with a large scope.

REFERENCES

- "Challenges in personalized systems for Personal Health Care" C.Fernández-Llatas Member, IEEE, A.Martinez-Romero, A.M. Bianchi Member IEEE, J.Henriques,P. Carvalho Member, IEEE, and V. Traver Member, IEEE978-1-5090-2455-1/16/$31.00 ©2016 IEEE.

- "Mining and Visualizing Associations of Concepts on a Large -scale Unstructured Data"Reza Sadoddin,Osvaldo Driollet, 2016 IEEE Second International Conference on Big Data Computing Serviceand Applications, 978-1-5090-2251-9/16 $31.00 © 2016 IEEE DOI 10.1109/BigDataService.2016.

- "Research and Improve on K-means Algorithm Based on Hadoop",Kehe Wu,Wenjing Zeng, Tingting Wu,Yanwen An, 978-1-4799-8353-7/15/$31.00 ©2015IEEE

- Xindong Wu, Fellow, IEEE, Xingquan Zhu "A Data Mining with Big Data", IEEE Transactions On Knowledge And Data Engineering, Vol. 26, No. 1, January 2014.

- Bo Liu, Member, IEEE, Keman Huang Jianqiang Li, and MengChu Zhou, "An Incremental and Distributed Infer-ence Method for Large-Scale Ontologies Based on MapReduce ParadigmKnowledge and InformationSystems", vol. 45, no. 3, pp. 603-630, Jan.2015.

- Muhammad MazharUllahRathore, Anand Paul "A Data Mining with Big Data" IEEE Transactions On Knowledge And Data Engineering, Vol. 26, No. 1, January 2014.

- Xindong Wu, Fellow, IEEE, Xingquan Zhu "Real-Time Big Data Analytical Architecturefor Remote Sensing Application-Knowledge and Information Systems", vol. 33, no. 3, pp 707-734, Dec. 2015.

- Yanfeng Zhang, Shimin Chen, Qiang Wang, and Ge Yu"MapReduce:Incremental MapReduce for Mining Evolving Big Data ACM Crossroads", vol. 27, no. 2, pp. July 2015.

- J. Mervis, "Science Policy: Agencies Rally to Tackle Big Data,Science", vol. 336, no. 6077, p. 22, 2012.

- D. Luo, C. Ding, and H. Huang "Parallelization with Mul-tiplicative Algorithms for Big Data Mining", IEEE 12th Intl-Conf. Data Mining, pp. 489-498, 2012.

- J. Bughin, M. Chui, and J. Manyika, "Clouds, Big Data, and Smart Assets: Ten Tech -Enabled Business Trendsto Watch.", McKinSey Quarterly, 2010.